Blue tit

A little bird with blue and yellow feathers. Watch for flocks of them darting around bird feeders in winter.

Garden snail

Snails need to stay moist, so they often come out to feed on plants at night, when the ground is cool and damp.

White clover

Grows low down, often among the grass on a lawn. You'll see bees visiting the flowers, which appear from May to October.

3

Paths and pavements

Common wasp

Don't panic if you see these striped insects buzzing around – they only sting when they feel threatened. April–October.

Dandelion

These grow in all kinds of places, even in tiny cracks in paths. Their golden flowers bloom from March to October.

Feral pigeon

You'll see flocks of these birds pecking on the ground, or perching high up along roofs and shop signs.

Urban Wildlife to Spot

Illustrated by Stephanie Fizer Coleman

Designed by Jenny Brown
Words by Kate Nolan

Note that the months given in the descriptions of some plants and animals in this book show the time of year when you're most likely to see them. If no months are mentioned, they can be spotted all year round.

In the garden

Red admiral butterfly

Look for this large insect fluttering around garden flowers on sunny days, even in winter.

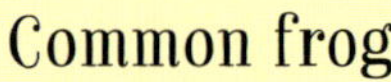

Common frog

You might find one resting in a shady, damp place, such as under leaves or near a log pile. February–October.

Robin

This bird is easy to spot thanks to its bright red feathers. Listen out for its cheerful song all year round.

Black ant

Thousands of them may live together
in nests under paving stones. Look for
their tiny tunnel entrances in the gaps
between the slabs. March–October.

Brown rat

Mostly lives underground,
but you might spot one
darting along looking for food
– it will eat almost anything.

Greater plantain

Search along path edges where
the tarmac has crumbled.
Its tall green flower spikes
appear from May to September.

In a park

Peacock butterfly

This large, dark red butterfly has blue and yellow spots on its wings that look like eyes, to scare off hunters.

Horse chestnut tree

Often grows very tall. Look for its pale flower spikes in April–May. Shiny brown 'conkers' (seeds) in spiky cases fall in autumn.

Wood pigeon

Looks similar to a feral pigeon (page 4) but bigger, with a white patch on its neck. Listen out for its raspy, cooing call.

Grey squirrel

Stay still and quiet when you see one scampering over the grass or along tree branches – it might come close.

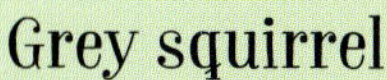

Ladybird

Look on rose bushes, where they might be feasting on aphids (tiny green or brown bugs). March–October.

Mallard

You'll see lots of these ducks paddling about on park ponds. Watch them diving down to find food under the water.

Around buildings

Giant crane fly

Gangly insects with long, fragile legs. You might see them fluttering around bright lights at night. April–October.

Ivy

Look for tendrils of this evergreen plant creeping up the outsides of buildings. It has flowers in autumn, and berries in winter.

House mouse

Lives wherever humans do, in holes and tunnels, especially in older buildings.

Starling

These noisy birds often gather in huge flocks – listen out for them making all kinds of whistling and trilling sounds.

House spider

If you see a cobweb in the corner of a room, it was probably made by one of these. They usually live in dark nooks near the floor.

Common orange lichen

Often grows in rounded patches, in all kinds of places – look on tree trunks, rocks, walls and fences.

City centre

London plane tree

Spot the bobble-shaped seed pods that stay on the tree through winter, and its patchy, peeling bark.

Male fern

Look on the tops of walls, in drains and other shady, damp places. Its long fronds might turn brown in autumn.

House sparrow

These little birds live in big groups, often making their nests under roofs or in holes in walls.

Magpie

Its black feathers gleam
blue-green as they catch the
light. Listen for its rattling,
'chacker-chacker' call.

Herring gull

Not just a seashore bird
– this big gull lives anywhere
it can scavenge for food waste
left by humans.

Yellow corydalis

You might see clumps of this
plant growing from cracks in
walls, or among stones and
gravel. May–October.

Ponds and canals

Coot

Spends most of its time on the water. Look for its white beak with a white 'shield' above it.

Mute swan

Large and graceful. It can dip down to eat pond plants from the bottom, thanks to its long, curved neck.

Large red damselfly

Watch for this bright insect resting on plants near the edge of the water. April–August.

Grey heron

You might see this tall bird standing very still at the water's edge, waiting to snap up a passing fish.

Moorhen

Similar to a coot, but its beak is red, with a yellow tip. Spot the white feathers under its tail.

Branched bur-reed

Tall, with long, pointed leaves, and greenish-white, spiky-looking flowers from April to August.

Empty ground

Chaffinch

Hops around under hedges hunting for seeds and insects. Try and spot the white feathers under its wings when it flies.

Blackberry

Dense tangles of this prickly plant can creep over big areas of ground. Watch for birds feasting on the berries in autumn.

Coltsfoot

You'll see its bright yellow flowers growing on scaly stems in March and April. Its leaves appear later in the spring.

Elder tree

Look for flat clusters of
creamy flowers in May and
June, and purple-black berries
in August–October.

Cinnabar moth

Flies during the day as well
as at night. Count the two
red spots on each of its
forewings. May–August.

Rosebay willowherb

You might find lots of these tall
plants growing together. Bright pink
flowers appear June–September.

Town streets

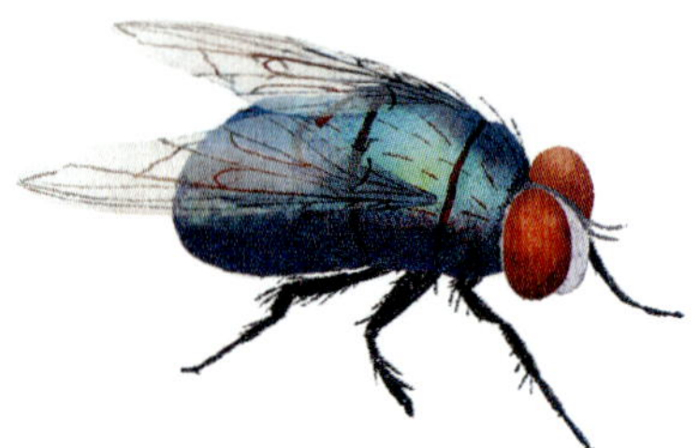

Blowfly

You might hear this large fly's loud, droning buzz near rubbish bins. It has a hairy, blue-green body. March–October.

Silver birch tree

Has a slender trunk, drooping branches and shiny, peeling bark. Look for catkins (long clusters of tiny flowers) in April.

Very common and easy to find

Shield lichen

You're most likely to see this silvery-green lichen growing on tree trunks or branches.

Pineapple weed

This feathery plant will grow almost anywhere. If you rub its leaves, you might smell its pineapple scent. June–September.

Swift

Listen for its piercing cry as it darts like an arrow high above the streets, catching insects in mid-air. April–September.

Sycamore tree

Its leathery leaves have jagged edges. Watch for the winged seeds spiralling in the air as they fall in autumn.

Hedges and verges

Blackbird

Hops around on grassy areas looking for insects and worms to eat. Listen for it singing as the sun begins to set.

English oak tree

Can grow very big and live for hundreds of years. Look for its wavy-edged leaves, and acorns growing in cups in autumn.

Daisy

This little plant is very easy to find all year round. It grows low to the ground, among short grasses.

Red mason bee

Lives alone rather than in a hive.
You might see it carrying little
bits of mud, which it uses to
make its nest. March–June.

Great tit

Similar to a blue tit (page 3)
but has a black head. Keep a
lookout for flocks of them
flying together in winter.

Common inkcap

Grows from old wood buried in
the ground. Remember NEVER
to touch any mushrooms you find
outside – some are poisonous.

Night-time

Hedgehog

This spiky little animal snuffles about in gardens and parks after dark, hunting for slugs. March–November.

Elephant hawk moth

Search for this large pink and gold moth at dusk, when it flutters around flowers such as honeysuckle. May–August.

Green lacewing

Watch for it flying near lights on summer evenings. It gets its name from its see-through wings. April–October.

Pipistrelle bat

Look up at twilight – you might just see
one darting through the sky, snapping
up flying insects. April–October.

Garden slug

There can be thousands of slugs
in a single garden! They spend
the daytime under the soil and
in other dark, damp places.

Red fox

Prowls town streets looking
for food waste left by humans.
Listen out for its screaming
cry on winter nights.

Spotting chart

Once you've spotted something from this book, find its sticker at the back, and stick it on this chart in the space below its name.

Black ant	Blackberry	Blackbird	Blowfly	Blue tit
Branched bur-reed	Brown rat	Chaffinch	Cinnabar moth	Coltsfoot
Common frog	Common inkcap	Common orange lichen	Common wasp	Coot
Daisy	Dandelion	Elder tree	Elephant hawk moth	English oak tree
Feral pigeon	Garden slug	Garden snail	Giant crane fly	Greater plantain

Great tit	Green lacewing	Grey heron	Grey squirrel	Hedgehog
Herring gull	Horse chestnut tree	House mouse	House sparrow	House spider
Ivy	Ladybird	Large red damselfly	London plane tree	Magpie
Male fern	Mallard	Moorhen	Mute swan	Peacock butterfly
Pineapple weed	Pipistrelle bat	Red admiral butterfly	Red fox	Red mason bee
Robin	Rosebay willowherb	Shield lichen	Silver birch tree	Starling
Swift	Sycamore tree	White clover	Wood pigeon	Yellow corydalis

Index

Black ant, 5
Blackberry, 14
Blackbird, 18
Blowfly, 16
Blue tit, 3
Branched bur-reed, 13
Brown rat, 5

Chaffinch, 14
Cinnabar moth, 15
Coltsfoot, 14
Common frog, 2
Common inkcap, 19
Common orange
   lichen, 9
Common wasp, 4
Coot, 12

Daisy, 18
Dandelion, 4

Elder tree, 15
Elephant hawk moth, 20
English oak tree, 18

Feral pigeon, 4

Garden slug, 21
Garden snail, 3
Giant crane fly, 8
Greater plantain, 5
Great tit, 19
Green lacewing, 20
Grey heron, 13
Grey squirrel, 7

Hedgehog, 20
Herring gull, 11
Horse chestnut tree, 6
House mouse, 8
House sparrow, 10
House spider, 9

Ivy, 8

Ladybird, 7
Large red damselfly, 12
London plane tree, 10

Magpie, 11
Male fern, 10
Mallard, 7
Moorhen, 13
Mute swan, 12

Peacock butterfly, 6
Pineapple weed, 17
Pipistrelle bat, 21

Red admiral
   butterfly, 2
Red fox, 21
Red mason bee, 19
Robin, 2
Rosebay willowherb, 15

Shield lichen, 16
Silver birch tree, 16
Starling, 9
Swift, 17
Sycamore tree, 17

White clover, 3
Wood pigeon, 6

Yellow corydalis, 11

First published in 2023 by Usborne Publishing Ltd, Usborne House, 83–85 Saffron Hill, London EC1N 8RT, England. usborne.com